PREHISTORIC ART
Cave Dwellers Edition
History for Kids

Asian, European, African, Americas & Oceanic Regions
4th Grade Social Studies

In this book, we're going to talk about prehistoric art around the world. So, let's get right to it!

WHAT IS PREHISTORIC ART?

One of the characteristics that distinguished early man from other primates was his use of art. Prehistoric art is art that was created from 200,000 BCE to 2000 BCE. Most of this art is rock art, but there are many different types, such as engravings, paintings, inscriptions, drawings, and carvings. All these types of rock art fall into two major categories:

- Petroglyphs
- Pictographs

PETROGLYPHS

Petroglyphs are engravings that have been carved into rock. This category also includes parietal art, which are sculptures created from the rock structures. Relief sculpture is one type of parietal art.

PREHISTORIC ROCK CARVING PETROGLYPHS ON STONE SURFACE, ALTA, NORWAY

PICTOGRAPHS

Pictographs are paintings or sketches done with pigments.

Stonehenge

A third type of art was composed of stones that were arranged by human hands into a monument. These were called megaliths or petroforms. Sometimes these stones were just small piles and at other times they were huge blocks of stone. Stonehenge in England, where massive stones are arranged in a circle, is one example of a famous megalith, dated to 2500 BCE. Another example is the Knowth Megalithic Tomb in Ireland, which dates to a similar time period as Stonehenge.

Both petroglyphs as well as pictographs have been discovered on cave walls and in outdoor areas where rocks are exposed. The earliest forms of this type of art found in Europe were created in underground caves. In the northern section of Africa, these forms of art have been discovered primarily on ground surfaces.

A LARGE CLIFF MURAL OF ANCIENT INDIAN
PETROGLYPHS AND PICTOGRAPHS

FREMONT PETROGLYPHS,
SEGO CANYON

Primitive societies used art to map or mark a territory, depict the stars and the heavens, make a record of important events, or to illustrate myths and spiritual beliefs.

HOW WERE PETROGLYPHS CREATED?

Prehistoric artists carved, scratched, sculpted, or drilled rock surfaces to create petroglyphs. Sometimes they used paint or dye on their engravings or they used tools to polish them. Petroglyphs have been found worldwide.

CROW CANYON PETROGLYPHS

S ome of the most famous examples have been found in
sections of Africa, in the northern and western regions
of Australia, in the southwestern region of North America,
in Siberia, in the country of Scandinavia, and on the Iberian
Peninsula.

PETROGLYPHS OF QOBUSTAN

For the most part, petroglyphs had very important significance for the artists who created them. They were deeply connected to the religion as well as the culture of the society that created them.

WHAT IS A CUPULE?

Perhaps one of the most mysterious types of petroglyphs is described as a cupule. It is the most ancient of all the forms of rock art. A cupule is an impression in the rock that has been pounded out in the shape of a rounded cup. Archaeologists don't know why prehistoric artists created these cupules, but they have been discovered on all the continents except for the continent of Antarctica.

CUPULE

PETROGLYPHS IN BHIMBETKA, INDIA

THE EARLIEST PETROGLYPHS

The earliest petroglyphs that have been found to date were discovered in the 1990s at the Auditorium Cave located in Bhimbetka and at Daraki-Chattan in a rock shelter. Both of these quartzite caves are located in India. The art consists of cupules and wavy engravings and it has been dated to 290,000 BCE.

Dating ancient pieces of art is a very difficult process. It requires high-tech equipment, but it also requires the knowledge of experts. The reason is that it's sometimes difficult to tell whether something is a natural rock formation or one that was created with human hands. However, once methods of dating become more advanced, it's possible that the Bhimbetka petroglyphs will be dated as far back as 700,000 BCE.

2 ELEPHANTS AND A MAN RIDING,
PRE HISTORIC BHIMBETKA ROCK CAVE PAINTINGS,
MADHYA PRADESH INDIA

The next oldest rock art engravings that have been found are in Blombos Cave in South Africa. The fragments of engraved rock that have been found there have geometric designs on them

and have been dated back to 70,000 BCE. They are the oldest such engravings that have been discovered on the African continent to date.

PETROGLYPHS COMBINED WITH PAINTING

As time went on, the artwork that primitive people created became more sophisticated. They used etching and carving and they also used painting. The images in the art expanded from cupules and simple geometric designs to realistic images of animals.

CHIRIBIQUETE PETROGLYPH

LIONS PAINTED IN THE
CHAUVET CAVE

S ome of the most famous and important prehistoric cave engravings are found at these locations, all in France:

CHAUVET CAVE

This cave was discovered in 1994, and contains some of the best primitive etchings and cave paintings dated to 30,000 BCE. There are thirteen different animal species including predatory animals, such as lions and bears. Some of the animals are shown in scenes with each other.

LE PLACARD CAVE

The art in the Le Placard cave dates to 17,500 BCE. Many of the images there are called aviforms because they are shapes that resemble birds. Some shapes appear to be antlers.

ROC-DE-SERS CAVE

This rock shelter is known for its rock engravings as well as its relief sculpture carved in limestone blocks. The animal figures depicted are bison, wild horses, and other animals. The rock art in this location has been dated to 17,200 BCE.

ROUFFIGNAC CAVE

This cave is known for its huge number of engravings of mammoths. It has an amazing ceiling with a swirling design of 60 drawings of horses, bison, and wild goats, which date to 14,000 BCE.

OLE DE L'AGE DU FER
(riode gauloise)
ROUFFIGNAC CAVE

VENUS OF LAUSSEL

RELIEF SCULPTURES

As primitive artists began to carve more deeply into rocks, their work became relief sculptures instead of etchings. The following examples are also located in France.

VENUS OF LAUSSEL

The Venus of Laussel is a relief sculpture. It is dated to 23,000 BCE and is a figure of an unclothed woman.

CAP BLANC ROCK SHELTER

The Cap Blanc Rock Shelter is known for its friezes carved into limestone. A frieze is a long, decorated panel. Prehistoric artists carved horses, bison, and reindeer into the rock walls there. Their art dates back to 15,000 BCE.

MARCASSITE CAP BLANC-NEZ

TUC D'AUDOUBERT BISONS

TUC D'AUDOUBERT CAVE

The Tuc d'Audoubert Cave is famous for its amazing bison relief sculptures, which were formed from clay that wasn't fired. The sculptures date back to 13,500 BCE.

HOW WERE PICTOGRAPHS CREATED?

Prehistoric artists created pictographs in one color and in many colors. They used pigments that came from natural chemicals, such as carbon as well as manganese and various oxides, which are rust-colored.

They used charcoal, pigments from clay soil, crushed bones from animals, animal blood, animal urine, juice from carrots and other berries, and other naturally available materials to create the different colors they wanted.

They were using these pigments for body painting long before they began to create pictures in caves.
PICTOGRAPHS AT PALATKI

Unfortunately for archaeologists, the paintings they created didn't withstand the passage of years as well as petroglyphs and relief sculptures did. Most of the pictographs that have survived were in

caves or outdoors in locations where there were protected by rocks that jutted out over the surfaces where they were drawn.

At the beginning, cave painters painted by using their fingers dipped into the pigments. Later they used brushes that were made with bristles from animals or tough plant fibers. They even developed more sophisticated techniques such as spraying paint on with reeds or hollow bones in a very early form of "airbrush style" painting.

All types of animals were depicted from the mighty mammoth, to the predatory lions and wolves, to the lowly wild hare. Hunting scenes were a common theme. When humans were drawn they were often simple stick figures or handprints. In fact, animals, abstract signs and symbols, and geometric designs appeared much more frequently than human figures.

Many of these symbols and designs in different cultures across the world became the basis for the first cuneiform characters and hieroglyphic characters. These characters eventually became the systems of writing in the ancient countries of China as well as Sumeria and Egypt. Art was the beginning of what would become another communication system—writing.

HIEROGLYPHIC

FREMONT PICTOGRAPH

FAMOUS PICTOGRAPHS

There are many famous pictographs on every continent except Antarctica. Here are some of the best known.

- Lascaux Cave Paintings, France
- Altamira Cave Paintings, Spain
- Kapova Cave Paintings, Russia

LASCAUX CAVE PAINTINGS, FRANCE

The Lascaux Cave Paintings have been dated to 17,000 BCE. This location is one of the most amazing examples of cave paintings worldwide with over 600 paintings of animals, such as black bulls and horses.

HORSE FROM LASCAUX CAVE

ALTAMIRA CAVE PAINTINGS, SPAIN

The Altamira Cave Paintings have been dated to 15,000 BCE or earlier and the site is known as the "Sistine Chapel" of the Stone Age era. It contains charcoal and multicolor paintings of animals and human hands.

KAPOVA CAVE PAINTINGS, RUSSIA

The Kapova Cave Paintings have been dated
to 12,500 BCE. This cave is famous for its rust-
colored mammoth paintings.

SUMMARY

Prehistoric rock art has been found on every continent except for Antarctica. These works of art were created between 200,000 BCE to 2,000 BCE, although some works are thought to be much older. Rock art falls into two major categories—petroglyphs and pictographs.

Awesome! Now that you've read about prehistoric art around the world, you may want to read about Native American art in the Baby Professor book

Native American Art - Art History Books for Kids | Children's Art Books.

Visit
BABY PROFESSOR
EDUCATION KIDS
www.BabyProfessorBooks.com
to download Free Baby Professor eBooks
and view our catalog of new and exciting
Children's Books